THE BLACK B∞K

A Practical Guide to Awaken Your Inner Genius

The Book of Proverbs and Ancient Wisdom
Paraphrased and Edited
by
DeCarlo A. Eskridge

NU DAE Enterprise Publications

United States of America

Copyright ©2012 by DeCarlo A. Eskridge, *NU DAE Enterprises, LLC. The Black Book*, A Practical Guide to Awaken Your Inner Genius

Unless otherwise indicated, all Scriptures paraphrased in this book of Proverbs are taken from the King James and the New King James Version of the Bible.

All rights reserved. No part of this publication may be reproduced, stored in a retrieval system or transmitted in any form or by any means electronic, mechanical, photocopying, recording or otherwise, without the prior written permission from the publisher, except by a reviewer who may quote brief passages in a review.

ISBN-13: 978-1469981871
ISBN-10: 1469981874

Edited by DeCarlo A. Eskridge
Cover Design ©NU DAE Enterprises, LLC, 2012
DeCarloEskridge.com

Printed in the United States of America

Contents

Contents v

Introduction vii

Being a Genius 1

The Power of Influence 7

The Abundant Life..11

Ask, Seek and Know 17

The Genius of Perseverance 21

Wisdom and Money 25

Overcoming Temptations..................................31

An Invitation to Wisdom 35

The Investigation of Wisdom 41

The Genius of Solomon 45

Gems of Genius 121

Additional Gems of Genius 133

Genius Insights 137

The Genius of Agur 167

The Genius of Kings 173

About the Author 181

Introduction

King Solomon, the son of David, was now in complete control of his kingdom, because the LORD God had blessed him and made him a powerful king.

Solomon loved the LORD and followed his father David's instructions; "Get wisdom and understanding!" Solomon also offered sacrifices and burned incense at the shrines. The most important shrine was in Gibeon, and Solomon had offered more than a thousand sacrifices on that altar, pleasing to the LORD.

One night while Solomon was in Gibeon, the LORD God appeared to him in a dream and said, "Solomon, ask for anything you want, and I will give it to you."

Solomon answered: My father David, your servant, was honest and did what you commanded. You were always loyal to him, and you gave him a son who is now king. LORD God, I am your servant, and you have made me king in my father's place. However, I am very young and know so little about being a leader. Now I must rule your chosen people, even though there are too many of them to count.

Please make me wise and teach me the difference between right and wrong. Then I will know how to rule your people. If you do not, there is no way I could rule this great nation of yours.

God said, "Solomon, I'm pleased that you asked for this. You could have asked to live a long time or to be rich. On the other hand, you could have asked for the lives of your enemies. Instead, you asked for **wisdom** to make right decisions. So I'll make you wiser than anyone who has ever lived or ever will live.

I will also give you what you did not ask for. You will be wealthy and respected as long as you live, and you'll be greater than any other king. If you obey me and follow my commands, as your father David did, I will bless you with wellness and long life."

Solomon woke up and realized that God had spoken to him in the dream. He went back to Jerusalem, "The City of David." There he offered sacrifices to pleasing to the Lord (1 Kings 3:1-15 & 2 Chronicles 1:1-13).

Solomon's Wisdom

Solomon was a genius. God had blessed him with insight and understanding. He was wiser than anyone else was in the world, including the wisest people of the east and of Egypt. Solomon wisdom was renown around the known world. Solomon wrote three thousand wise sayings and composed more than one thousand songs. He could talk about all kinds of plants, from large trees to small bushes, and he taught about animals, birds, reptiles, and fish. Kings and world's wealthiest people would travel from near and far to listen to the teaching of Solomon (1 Kings 11:29-34).

Solomon's Wealth

Solomon received about twenty-five tons of gold a year. The merchants and traders, as well as the kings of Arabia and rulers from Israel, also gave him gold (2 Chronicles 9:13-14).

Solomon made two hundred gold shields and used about seven and a half pounds of gold for each one. He also made three hundred smaller gold shields, using almost four pounds for each one, and he put the shields in his palace in Forest of Lebanon (2 Chronicles 9:15-16).

His throne was made of ivory and covered with pure gold. The back of the throne was rounded at the top, and it had armrests on each side. There was a statue of a lion on both sides of the throne, and there was a statue of a lion at both ends of each of the six steps leading up to the throne. No other throne in the world was like Solomon. Since silver was almost worthless in those days; everything was made of gold, even the cups and dishes used in the House of the Forest of Lebanon were of pure gold Solomon had a fleet of trading ships. Every three years he sent them out with Hiram's ships to bring back gold, silver, and ivory, as well as monkeys and peacocks (2 Chronicles 9:17-21).

He was the richest and wisest king in the world. People from every nation wanted to hear the wisdom God had given him. Every year people came bringing gifts of silver and gold, as well as clothes, weapons, spices, horses, or mules (2 Chronicles 9:22-24).

Solomon had one thousand four hundred chariots and twelve thousand horses that he kept in Jerusalem and other towns. While he was king, there was silver everywhere in Jerusalem, and cedar was as common as ordinary sycamore trees in the foothills. Solomon's merchants bought his horses and chariots as well, paying about fifteen pounds of silver for a chariot and almost four pounds of silver for a horse. They also sold horses and chariots to the Hittite and Syrian kings (2 Chronicles 9:25-28).

Solomon Dies

However, in spite of the great advantages of his heritage from David, wisdom from God, and the prosperity and security that resulted, late in life Solomon turned from following God and lived a life full of sin. His wives turned away his imagination after other gods; and his imagination was not perfect with Lord his God, as the imagination of David his father. As a result, the glory days of Israel were short-lived.

Then the Lord took away His blessing from Solomon, and riots and rebellions began against him among the Hebrew people. Solomon understood that this was God's punishment for his sins and began to repent. However, he did not fully surrender his heart to the Lord his God as his father David had done. Therefore, although the Lord forgave him and preserved his kingdom during his life, still He announced through a prophet that after the death of Solomon the Israelite kingdom would be split in two, and Solomon's son would inherit the smaller part.

Everything else Solomon did while he was king is written in the books about him and his wisdom. After he had ruled forty years from Jerusalem, he died and was buried there in the city of his father David. His son Rehoboam then became king (2 Chronicles 9:29-31).

For your convenience, notes pages have been added at the end of each chapter.

Chapter 1

Being a Genius

These are the wise sayings of Solomon, son of David, king of Israel: They will instruct you in the spirit of genius, understanding wisdom, and wise teaching. They will aid you in your quest to discover the ways of wisdom, wellness, and wealth. They give wisdom to those who possess childlike faith and much learning and wisdom to those who seek personal evolution. A conscious creator will hear and grow in learning. A person of understanding will be able to understand a wise saying, a proverb, the words of the wise, and their meanings. [1-6]

The acknowledgment of Divine Intelligence is the beginning of consciousness. The unconscious creator abhors wisdom and wise teaching. [7]

Exhortations to Embrace Wisdom

Obey your parent's teaching, my child, and do not turn away from them, for they will be a crown of glory to your head and a beautiful chain around your neck. [8-9]

My child, if unconscious people attempt to lead you down a wrong path do not follow them. If they say, "Come with us. Let us go out and harm someone. Let us set a trap for those who have done us no wrong. Let us eat them alive like a cancer, as those who go down to the grave. We will steal all kind things worth a lot of money. We will fill our houses with the stolen goods. Join us. We will split the money equally." My child, do not follow them. Keep your feet from their path, for they pursue after harmful devices, and they are quick to destroy life. It is futile to spread a net while a bird is watching. They set traps for their own lives and wait to die. Such are the ways of all who acquire wealth by harming others. Their desire for stolen riches will destroy them. 10-19

Consequences of Rejecting Wisdom

Wisdom calls out in the street. She lifts her voice in the center of town. There she cries out in the noisy streets. In the city square she speaks: "You who are without understanding how long will you love your unconsciousness? How long will you take pleasure in the misfortune of others? How long will the ignorant hate learning? Listen to my strong words! See, I will pour out my Spirit on you. I will make my words known to you. I called but you would not listen. I put out my hand and no one gave it a thought. You did not listen when I told you what you should do, and you would not heed any of my corrections. Therefore, I will laugh in your time of calamity. I will laugh when fear overtakes your mind. Fear will come to you like a great storm. Hard times will come like a strong wind. I will laugh when trouble and suffering thrashes your door. 20-27

Then you will call on me, but I will not answer. You will look for me, but you will not find me, because you hated my instruction, and did not choose to esteem your Creator. You would not listen when I told you what you should do. You laughed at my counsel and scorned my rebuke. Therefore, you will eat the fruit of your actions, and experience the consequences of your own ignorance. For the unwise are destroyed because of their lack of understanding. The trust they place in themselves will destroy them. But the person who trusts me will be protected from danger, and he will rest easy from the fear of harm." 28-33

Divine Insights

Chapter 2

The Power of Influence

My child, follow my teachings and treasure my instructions. Keep in tune with wisdom and understand what it means to exercise good judgment. Cry aloud for good sense. Search for wisdom as you would search for silver or hidden treasure. Then you will understand what it means to reverence and to know Divine Intelligence. All wisdom comes from Him, and so does common sense and understanding. Divine Intelligence gives helpful advice to everyone who obeys Him and protects all of those who acknowledge Him. He watches over all who think and behave appropriately, and He preserves everyone who is faithful to Divine Law. [1-8]

Then you will understand what is right and good, and right from wrong and you will know what to do at any given moment. For wisdom will pour forth from the inner most part of your being. Moreover, much learning will be pleasing to your soul. Right thinking will watch over you. Understanding will protect you. [9-11]

You will be protected from the depraved person and the troublemaker who talks too much. You will be protected from the person who walks in the ways of thoughtless, from the one who takes pleasure in doing wrong, and who finds joy in perverse behavior. His ways are perverted and not beneficial. 12-15

Genius of Self-Control

Wisdom will protect you from the seductive woman with her skillful tongue, who has left the husband of her youth and ignored the wedding vows she made before her Creator. The road to her house leads down to the dark world of utter unconsciousness. Visit her, and you will never find the road of life again. 16-19

Live in your integrity. If you are honest and live according to these principles, you will prosper in all you do. However, if you are ignorant, you alone will suffer the consequences. 20-22

Divine Insights

Chapter 3

The Abundant Life

My child, do not forget my teaching. Meditate upon my words in your heart (*subconscious mind*), for they will prolong your life and bring you prosperity. 1-2

Forsake not love and truth; let them be a gold chain around your neck, engrave them upon your mind. Then you will have good success, favor in the sight of Divine Intelligence and all of His creation. 3-4

Trust in Divine Intelligence with all your heart, soul, mind, and strength. Do not rely on your own limited reasoning power; in all your ways acknowledge Him, and He will show you the absolute best path to take. 5-6

Do not be wise in your own conceit. Respect Divine Intelligence and turn away from erroneous thinking. It will be healing to your body and medicine to your bones. Honor your Creator with your wealth, and with the first fruits of your labor. Then your houses will be filled with many good things and over flowing with abundances. 7-10

My child, listen when Divine Intelligence speaks to you, do not loose heart when He corrects you. The Creator disciplines everyone He loves, as a father corrects the ones who bring him joy. 11-12

The Value of Wisdom

Prosperous is the person who discovers his individual genius (*wisdom*) and seeks the best means to employ it. For wisdom is better than getting silver and fine gold. She is worth more than priceless diamonds. Nothing you can wish for compares with her. Long life (*wellness*) is in her right hand. Riches (*wealth*) and honor are in her left hand. Her ways are pleasing, and all her paths are peaceful. She is a tree of life to those who take hold of her. Prosperous are all who embrace her. 13-18

By His innate genius, Divine Intelligence laid the foundation of the earth. By wisdom, He rolled out the heavens. By His infinite knowledge, the seas were divided and rain falls from the sky. 19-20

My child, use common sense and sound judgment! Always keep them in mind. They will help you to live a long and prosperous life; they will be chain of beauty around your neck. Then you will be safe as you walk on your way, and your foot will not slip. You will not be afraid when you sleep. When you lie down, your sleep will be sweet. Do not be afraid of sudden disaster or of the calamity, that over takes the unconscious creator. For Divine Intelligence will be your protection. It will keep your foot from slipping. [21-26]

Do not withhold good from those who deserve it, when it is in your power to give it. Do not put off until tomorrow the good you are capable of today. [27-28]

Do not conspire to harm your neighbor, while he lives safely beside you. Do not falsely accuse a person for no reason, when he has done you no harm. [29-30]

Do not envy a violent person or follow his example. Divine Intelligence abhors a deceitful person, but He is close to those who think and behave appropriately. [31-32]

Divine Law does not favor the house of the double-minded person, but it prospers the house of those who thinks with singleness of purpose. [33]

Divine Intelligence laughs at those who laugh at His wisdom but gives loving kindness to those who are humble of heart. The conscious inherit wisdom, wellness, and wealth but lack, loss, and limitations will be the inheritance of the unwise. 34-35

Divine Insights

Chapter 4

Ask, Seek, and Know

My child, hear the teaching of a parent. Listen so you may obtain understanding. For I give you sound teaching. Do not turn away from it. When I was a much loved and only child of my mother and father, he taught me, saying, "Keep my words close to your heart (*subconscious mind*). Keep my teachings and live. Get wisdom and understanding. Do not forget or turn away from the words of my mouth. Do not leave her alone, and she will keep you safe. Love her, and she will watch over you. Get wisdom! And with all you have gotten, get understanding. Honor her and she will honor you. She will honor you if you hold her close to your heart (*subconscious mind*); meditate on her day and night. She will adorn your head with a crown of loving-favor and beauty." [1-9]

Hear, my child, and receive my sayings, and the years of your life will be prolonged. I have instructed you in the ways of genius. I have led you on the right paths. When you walk, you will not stumble. If you run, you will not fall. Take hold of wisdom, do not let her go. Watch over her, for she is your life. Do not go on the path of the unconscious. Do not walk in the way of corrupt person. Stay away from it. Do not pass by it. Turn from it, and pass on. The unconscious cannot sleep unless they are practicing deceit. They are robbed of sleep unless they make someone stumble. For they eat the bread of disobedience, and drink the wine of the poorly behaved. However, the way of those who think and behave appropriately is like the early morning sun. It shines brighter and brighter with each passing day. The way of the unconscious is like deep darkness; they do not know what causes them to stumble. 10-19

My child, pay attention to what I say; listen closely to my words. Do not let them out of your sight; mediate on them daily. For they are life to those who find them, and healing to the body. Keep your heart (*subconscious mind*) pure for out of it flow the issues of life. Put deceitful speaking away from you. Put away perverse speech far from your mouth. Let your eyes look straight ahead, and keep focused on what is in front of you. Keep a watch over your behavior; establish your ways. Do not turn to the right or to the left. Stay on the right track. 20-27

Divine Insights

Chapter 5

The Genius of Perseverance

My child, listen to my wisdom. Turn your ear to my words. So you may know what right thinking is, and your lips may speak much knowledge. For the lips of a seductive person are as sweet as honey. Their talk is as smooth as oil. But in the end they are as bitter tasting as wormwood, and as sharp as a two edge sword. Their feet go down to death. Their steps take hold of the grave. They do not think about the path of life. Their path is unstable, and they do not realize it. [1-6]

Now then, my child, listen to me. Do not turn away from the words of my mouth. Keep away from the seductive person. Do not go near the door of their house. If you do, you would give your strength to another, and your years to those without loving-kindness. [7-9]

Strangers would be filled with your strength, and the rewards of your labor would go to a stranger's house. You would cry inside yourself when your end comes, when your flesh and body are wasted away. You would say, "How I have hated teaching!

My soul hated strong correction! I have not listened to the voice of my teachers. I have not turned my ear to those who would teach me. Now my name is disgraced among the people." 10-14

Drink water in your own house, my child be faithful to your spouse. Why should you give your affections to a stranger on the street? Let your children be yours alone, and not a stranger on the street. Be pleased and rejoice with the spouse you have married. Be satisfied with your spouse's body and sweet embrace. Why take pleasure in a stranger, or embrace what can never be yours? 15-20

A person's ways are transparent before the eyes of the Lord, and He knows the intent of the heart. The misdeeds of the deceitful person will ensnare him. He will be imprisoned by the imagination of his own thoughts. He will perish due to a lack of understanding, and will stray off course because of the depth of his unconsciousness. 21-23

Divine Insights

Chapter 6

Wisdom and Money

My child, if you have become cosigner for a friend, if you have struck your hands in pledge for a stranger; you are trapped by the words of your lips. You are ensnared with the words of your mouth. Do this now, my child, and get yourself out of the agreement, for you have become collateral for your friend. Swallow your pride and beg your friend to release you from the contract of your words. Do it now. Do not rest until you do. If possible, flee for your life, save yourself like a deer that escapes from a hunter or a bird from the net. 1-5

Learn a lesson from the ant, you lazy person. Observe their ways and be wise. They have no leader, head or ruler, but they get their food ready in the summer, and gather their food for the winter. How long will you sleep, you lazy person? When will you wake up? A little sleep, a little rest, a little idleness, and poverty will overtake you like a burglar, and your need like a mugger. 6-11

A worthless person goes around deceiving others. They are always thinking up harmful schemes and stirring up trouble. However, they will be struck by sudden disaster and left without a hope or a prayer. 12-15

There are six things which the Creator hates, yes, seven that are despised by Him: A proud look, a lying tongue, and hands that kill the innocent, a heart that entertains destructive desires, feet that are swift in running to mischief, a person who tells lies about someone else, and one who causes dissension among acquaintance. 16-19

The Perils of Infidelity

My child, obey the teaching of your parents. Keep them close to your heart (*subconscious mind*). Wear them around your neck like a chain of gold. They will guide throughout your life. They will watch over you when you sleep, and they will talk with you when you wake up. For the word is a lamp. Sound teaching is a light and strong words provide direction in the way of life. 20-23

These words and this teaching will keep you from the perfidious person, from the smooth tongue of the adulterous. Do not lust after her beauty. Don't let her coyness seduce you. A prostitute will bring you to poverty, and sleeping with someone else's spouse will cost you your life. Can you walk on hot coals and not be burned? So it is with the person who sleeps with another person's spouse. He who embraces her will experience the negative results of his action. 24-29

People may excuse a thief who steals because he is hungry. But if he is caught, he will be fined seven times as much as he stole, even if it means selling everything in his house to pay it back. However, the person who commits adultery is a complete idiot, for he destroys his own life. Wounds and constant disgrace will be his plight in life. His shame will never be erased. For the woman's husband will be furious in his jealousy, and he will have no mercy in his day of vengeance. He will not take a bribe, and he will not be persuaded no matter what is offered him. 30-35

Divine Insights

Chapter 7

Overcoming Temptations

My child, pay close attention and do not forget what I tell you to do. Obey my word and you will live! Let my instructions be your greatest treasure. Tie them around your fingers. Write them upon your heart (*subconscious mind*). Say to wisdom, "You are my sister." Call understanding your best friend. They will keep you from the strange woman, from the stranger with her smooth words. 1-5

I looked out through the window of my house and I saw among the naïve and among the immature a young man without wisdom and understanding. He passed through the street near the seductive woman's corner and took the path to her house, in the light of the evening, after it was dark. 6-9

See, a woman comes to meet him. She is dressed like a prostitute, and with the intentions to deceive and entrap someone. She is loud and has a strong self-will. Her feet do not stay at home. She is now in the street, now in the center of town where people gather.

She lies in wait at every corner. She embraces him and kisses him. With a serious face, she says to him, "It was time for me to give gifts on the altar in worship, and today I have paid what I promised. So I have come out to meet you, to look for you, and I have found you. I have covered my bed with linen cloth from Egypt. I have perfumed my bed with fine perfumes and spices. Come, let us make love all night long; let us delight ourselves with love. For my husband is not at home. He has gone on a long business trip. He has taken a suitcase full of money with him, and he will not return for several weeks." Therefore, she deceived him with all of her sweet talk and the flattery of her lips. Right away, he followed her like an ox on its way to the slaughterhouse, or like an unconscious creator about to be ambush and put to death. He was no more than a bird rushing into a trap, without knowing it would cost him his life. 10-23

My son, pay close attention to what I have said. Do not let your thoughts turn aside to her ways; do not stray into her paths. Many are those she has placed in the grave, and her victims are innumerable. Her house is the way to grave, going down to the chambers of death. 24-27

Divine Insights

Chapter 8

An Invitation to Wisdom

Does not wisdom call? Does not understanding raise her voice? She takes her stand on the top of the hill beside the way, where the roads meet. Beside the gates in front of the town, at the open doors, she cries out, "I call to you, people. My voice is to the children of men. Naive children, learn to use wisdom. You, who are ignorant, open your mind to wisdom. Listen, for I will teach you great things. What is right will come from my lips. For my mouth will speak the truth. My lips abhor that which is contrary to truth. All the words of my mouth are right and good. There is nothing in my lips that speaks against the truth. They are all clear to them who understand, and right to those who find much learning. Seek my teaching instead of silver. Seek much learning instead of fine gold. For wisdom is better than jewels of great worth. There is nothing in the world that compares to the value gain from wisdom." [1-11]

"I, wisdom, live with understanding, and I find much learning and careful thinking. The love of Divine Law is to hate what is contrary to the law. I hate pride, selfishness, perversion, and lies. I have instructions and wisdom. I have understanding and power. I cause leaders to lead and rulers to disperse justice. By me rulers rule and great people execute judgment on the earth. I love those who love me, and those who diligently seek me will find me. With me are riches and honor, enduring wealth and prosperity. My fruit is better than gold, even pure gold. What I give is better than fine silver. I walk in the way that acknowledges God, in the center of the ways that are fair. I give wealth to those who love me, and fill their vault with treasures." 12-21

"Divine Intelligence conceived me at the beginning of His work, before His first works long ago. I was set apart long ago, from the beginning, before the earth was. I was born when there were no seas, when there were no pools full of water. I was born before the mountains and hills were in their places. I was before He had made the earth or the fields, or the first dust of the world. I was there when He made the heavens, and when He drew a mark around the top of the sea. I was there when He framed the skies above, and when He put the wells of the waters in their place. I was there when He marked the boundary for the sea, so that the waters would not go farther than what He decreed. I was there when He marked out the ground for the earth. I was beside Him as the leading craftsman. I was His joy every day. I rejoiced in His presence and delight in humanity." 22-31

"So my children listen to me, for prosperous are they who keep my ways. Hear my teaching and be wise. Do not turn away from it. Prosperous is the one who listens to me, watching every day at my gates, waiting patiently beside my doors. For whoever finds me finds life, and gets favor from Divine Intelligence. But those who dismiss me injure themselves; all who love ignorance seeks their own ruin." 32-36

Divine Insights

Chapter 9

The Investigation of Wisdom

Wisdom has built her house. She has secured it with seven pillars. She has cooked her food, and has mixed her wine, and she has set her table. She has sent out the young women who work for her. She calls from the highest places of the city, "Whoever is easy to deceive let him turn in here!" She says to the one without understanding, "Come and eat my food, and drink the wine I have mixed. Turn from your ignorant way, and live. Walk in the way of understanding." [1-6]

He who speaks strong words to the person who is ignorant and laughs at the truth brings shame upon himself. He who speaks strong words to a person of little understanding does so at his own expense. Do not correct a person who is not teachable or he will laugh at the truth, and he will despise you. Speak strong words to a conscious creator, and he will love you. Teach a wise person and he will be even wiser. Teach a person who has understanding, and he will grow in learning. The awe of Divine Intelligence is the beginning of wisdom. To grow in the knowledge of the

Holy One is understanding. For by me your days will grow in number, and years will be added to your life. If you are wise, your wisdom benefits you. On the other hand if you laugh at the truth, you alone will pay the consequences. 7-12

The Wages of Ignorance

The willful woman is loud; she is ignorant and knows nothing. She sits at the door of her house, on a seat in the high places of the city. She calls to those who pass by and who are headed in the right direction, "Whoever is easy to deceive, let him turn in here!" She says to the one who lacks understanding, "Stolen water is sweet. And bread eaten in secret is pleasing." However, he does not know that the dead are there, and that the ones who visit her are in the grave. 13-18

Divine Insights

Chapter 10

The Genius of Solomon

The wise sayings of Solomon: A wise child makes a father glad, but an ignorant child brings sorrow to his mother. [1]

Wealth gain by deceit profits little, but right living will preserve you. [2]

The Creator will not let those who place their trust Him go without any good thing, but He overthrows the desire of the faithless. [3]

The lazy person will be impoverished, but diligent hands bring wealth. [4]

A person who gathers in summer is wise, but a person who sleeps during harvest time experience shame. [5]

Great results are the byproduct of those who think and behave appropriately before Divine Intelligence, but the mouth of the deceitful conceals lies. [6]

Those who think and behave appropriately before the Creator are honored, but the name of the deceitful person will not be remembered. [7]

The wise in heart (*subconscious mind*) will grow in knowledge, but the ignorant person who is quick to speak will perish. 8

Whoever walks in his integrity walks securely, but whoever follows perverse ways will be discovered. 9

He who winks his eye causes trouble, but the one who rebukes boldly makes peace. 10

The mouth of the one who behaves wisely before his Creator is a fountain of life, but the mouth of the undisciplined conceals trouble. 11

Hatred starts fights, but love covers a multitude of sins. 12

Wisdom is discovered in the mouth of those who have understanding, but correction is for him who lacks understanding. 13

The wise increases in knowledge, but the unconscious will be destroyed by the words of their own mouths. 14

The wealth of a rich person is his strength, but the impoverished person's mindset will destroys him. 15

The wealth earned by those who think and behave appropriately before their Creator increase life, but the corrupt are rewarded by their actions. [16]

He who receives instruction is on the right road of life, but he who will not listen to correction is lost. [17]

Deceitful lips conceal hatred, and he who speaks slander is without understanding. [18]

When words are many, indiscretion is certain, but the conscious creator restrains his speech against idle words. [19]

The tongue of those who acknowledge their Creator is like fine silver, but the thoughts of the unconscious are worthless. The lips of those who acknowledge their Creator feed many, but fools lips are improvised for want of understanding. [20-21]

The understanding of Divine Law makes one rich, and adds no sorrow. [22]

Being mischievous is child's play to the unconscious, but a person of understanding has wisdom. [23]

The fears of the fearful will overtake take him, and desire of the faithful will be manifested. [24]

When hard times pass, the fearful are no more, but the faithful are established forever. 25

Like a lemon in the month, and smoke to the eyes, so are the lazy to those who employee them. 26

The respect of Divine Law extends one's life; the years of the faithless are reduced. 27

The hope of faithful is fulfilled, but the expectation of the faithless will diminished. 28

The way of Divine Law is a safe haven to those who believe, but unconscious will perish. 29

Those who place their trust in Divine Intelligence will never be moved, but the unfaithful will not manifest their desire. 30

The mouth of the upright brings forth wisdom, but the perverse tongue will be silence. 31

The lips of those who think and behave appropriately before their Creator speak what is pleasing to others, but the mouth of the perverse speaks only lies. 32

Divine Insights

Chapter 11

The Creator despises false scales, but an accurate weight is His delight. 1

Shame follows pride, but with humility comes wisdom. 2

The integrity of the upright shall guide them, but the perversion of the unfaithful will be their destruction. 3

Wealth is of no use in the Day of Judgment, but living right before your Creator will save you from ruin. 4

Those who think and behave appropriately before their Creator are without blame, making their path straight, but the unfaithful will fall by their own misdeeds. 5

Living right before the Creator will save the person of integrity, but those who harm others will be trapped by their own selfish desires. 6

When a vile person dies, his hope dies with him, and all his power amounts to nothing. 7

The person who behaves wisely before his Creator is protected from trouble and the selfish person takes his place. [8]

The deceitful person destroys his neighbor with his mouth, but those who are upright will be saved through knowledge of Supreme Intelligence. [9]

The city prospers when its leaders think and behave appropriately before the Creator, and there are shouts of joy when tyrants perish. [10]

A city is honored by the good that come to the faithful, but the mouth of the perverse destroys it. [11]

He who hates his neighbor is void of understanding, but a person of understanding maintains his peace. [12]

A gossiper makes secrets known, but he who is faithful keeps secrets. [13]

Where there is no guidance, a nation falls, but in an abundance of counselors, there is safety. [14]

To secure a loan for a stranger guarantees trouble, but whoever refuses to cosign for another lives secured. [15]

A woman full of grace is honored, but an undisciplined woman is covered with shame: those who despise work will experience lack, but the diligent increase in wealth. [16]

The person who shows loving-kindness manifest good, but the person without mercy will destroy himself. [17]

The unfaithful person earn dishonest wages; but his reward is certain who plants the seeds of a conscientious lifestyle. [18]

Whoever thinks right will prosper, but whoever pursues perverse thoughts will perish. [19]

Divine Intelligence does not prosper those who are perverse in their thoughts, but takes pleasure in those who think and behave appropriately. [20]

The perverse person experiences the consequences of his perversion, but Divine Intelligence protects all who think and behave appropriately. [21]

A beautiful woman without good sense is like a gold ring in the nose of a pig. [22]

The desire of a good person is established. The expectation of the perverse fades away. [23]

A person gives freely, and his wealth is multiplied; however, another person withholds and becomes impoverished. 24

The person who gives much will have an abundance, and he who helps others will prosper. 25

The people curse those who withhold good, but a blessing is on the head of those who give it freely. 26

He who looks for good obtains favor, but he who looks for trouble will surely find it. 27

He who trusts in his wealth will fall, but those who behave wisely before their Creator will prosper like a tree of life. 28

He who troubles his own house will inherit the wind, and the ignorant will be employed by those with understanding. 29

The fruit of right living is a tree of life, he who is wise wins favor but those who practice violence are destroyed. 30

If right thinking manifest after its kind in the natural realm, how much more will perverse and unconscious thoughts manifest after their kind? 31

Divine Insights

Chapter 12

Whoever loves correction loves learning, but whoever hates correction is an idiot. [1]

A sensible person will gain favor from Divine Law, but it is a crude instructor for those who behaves poorly. [2]

A person will not succeed by doing what is wrong, but those who think and behave appropriately before their Creator will prosper. [3]

A good wife is the pride and joy of her husband, but she who brings shame is like cancer to his bones. [4]

The thoughts of those who think and behave appropriately before their Creator can be trusted, but the words of the unfaithful are deceptive. [5]

The words of the unconscious lie in wait for blood, but the mouth of the conscious will protect them from trouble. [6]

The unconscious are destroyed and are no more, but the house of those who think and behave appropriately before Their Maker will endure forever. [7]

A person is praised for his genius, but a person with a perverse mindset is despised. 8

A humble person with a single pupil is better than the impoverished with an air of self-importance. 9

A person who unites himself with Supreme Intelligence cares for his animal, but even the unconscious creator's kindness is cruel. 10

He who works with his hands prospers, but he who chases get rich schemes lacks understanding. 11

The corrupt person attracts corruption, but the manifestation of those who think and behave appropriately is good. 12

The perverse person is trapped by his words of his month, but those who think and behave appropriately before their Creator are safe. 13

A conscious creator's words will bring him abundance, and the work of his hands will increase his wealth. 14

The unconscious creator is wise in his own eyes, but the conscious creator listens to sound advice. 15

The unconscious creator's anger is known immediately, but a conscious creator holds her peace when criticized. [16]

The person who speaks truth tells what is right, but a liar tells lies. [17]

The unconscious creator's words cuts like a knife, but the tongue of the conscious creator brings healing. [18]

Words of truth endure forever. However, a liar's words last for an instant. [19]

Deceit is in the heart of those who practice deception, but those who do what is right have joy. [20]

No trouble comes to those who think and behave appropriately before their Maker, but the lives of the unconscious are filled with difficulty. [21]

Divine Intelligence abhors lying lips, but those who speak truth are His delight. [22]

A conscious creator conceals what he knows, but the unconscious creator pours out his heart. [23]

The hands of the diligent will become great, but the lazy person will be made his servant. [24]

Anxious thoughts weigh a person down. However, an encouraging word lifts him up. 25

The person who behaves wisely before his Creator will teach his neighbor, but the corrupt person will encounter adversity. 26

The lazy person will not cook the food he has purchased, but the diligent person takes pleasure in his labor. 27

The Creator increases the lives of those who think and behave appropriately, and they should live forever. 28

Divine Insights

Chapter 13

A conscious child listens when his parent tells him the right way, but one who laughs at the truth does not listen when he is corrected. 1

From the goodness of his mouth a man experiences wisdom, wellness, and wealth, but the hurtful person experiences lack, loss, and limitations. 2

He who watches over his mouth keeps his life, but he who opens his mouth hastily will perish. 3

The soul of the lazy person has many desires but gets nothing, but the soul of the diligent receives more than she expects. 4

A conscious creator abhors lies, but the unconscious person experiences the shame of their own behavior. 5

Good behavior protects the innocent, but the perverse are destroyed by their own devices. 6

There is one who pretends to be rich, but has nothing. Another pretends to be poor, but has great wealth. 7

A rich person can use his riches to ransom his life, but no one threatens a poor person's life. 8

Those who acknowledge their Creator are full of light, but the lamp of the unconscious will be extinguished. 9

Contentions come only from pride, but wisdom is with those who listen when told what they should do. 10

Wealth obtain by dishonest means is quickly lost, but the hands of the diligent shall prosper. 11

Hope that is put off makes the heart sick, but a desire that is manifested into existence is a fountain of life. 12

He who hates the Word will be destroyed, but he who esteems the Word will prosper. 13

The teaching of an enlighten person is a fountain of life, to save one from the pitfalls in life. 14

Good understanding wins favor, but the decisions of the unconscious is painful. 15

Every conscious creator acts with much knowledge, but the unconscious creator makes his shameful ways known. 16

An unreliable colleague falls into trouble, but a faithful colleague brings healing. [17]

He who will not listen to correction will become impoverished, but he who listens when corrected will prosper. [18]

A desire that is fulfilled is sweet to the soul, but an idiot hates to give up even that which is detrimental to his life. [19]

He who surrounds himself with wise people will be wise, but the companion of fools will suffer. [20]

Trouble follows the unconscious, but good things will overtake those who think and behave appropriately before their Creator. [21]

A good person leaves an inheritance for his children's children. The wealth of the unconscious is stored up for the conscious. [22]

Much food is in the cultivated land of the poor, but it is taken away because of a lack of justice. [23]

He who does not correct his child is not showing love, but he who loves his child will correct him promptly. [24]

The good person eats to live, while the greedy person lives to eat. [25]

Divine Insights

Chapter 14

The conscious woman builds up her house, but the unconscious woman tears her house down. [1]

He who walks honorably respects Divine Law, but the unconscious abhors it. [2]

An unconscious creator is ensnared by his conversation, but the lips of the conscious creator will protect him. [3]

There is no manure where there are no oxen, but a great harvest comes by the strength of the ox. [4]

A faithful person speaks the truth, but the unfaithful person tells lies. [5]

One who laughs at the truth looks for wisdom and finds it not, but understanding comes easy to him who is open to the truth. [6]

Depart from the presence of an ignorant person, when you perceive he lacks the words of knowledge. [7]

The genius of the conscious creator is planning, but the unconscious creator refuses to face reality. [8]

The ignorant laugh at inappropriate behavior, but the favor of the Creator is among the faithful. 9

The heart knows its own is bitterness, and a stranger cannot share its joy. 10

The house of the unconscious will be destroyed, but wisdom, wellness, and wealth are in the house of the conscious. 11

There is a way which appears right to a person, but its end is the way of death. 12

Even while laughing the heart may be in pain. The end of joy is often sorrow. 13

The person who repeats a nasty habit will be rewarded by the fruits of his actions, and a good person will be compensated by the fruits of his actions. 14

The one who is easily deceived believes everything, but the conscious creator looks before she leaps. 15

The conscious creator honors his Creator and turns away from danger, but the unconscious moves ahead in his arrogance. 16

He who has a quick temper acts hastily, and the plans of the unconscious are despised. 17

The unconscious are easily deceived, but the conscious understand Divine Law. [18]

Unconscious creator will revere the conscious creator, and wait outside the door of those who understand Divine Law. [19]

The impoverished person is even despised by his neighbor, but the rich person has many friends. [20]

He who hates his neighbor is in error, but prosperous is he who shows loving-kindness to the poor. [21]

Do not those who make unconscious plans take the wrong paths in life? Kindness and truth are for those who choose the right paths in life. [22]

In all work, there is some benefit, but talk is cheap. [23]

The conscious creator experiences the positive results of Divine Law, but an unconscious creator experience the negative results of his own thinking. [24]

The words of the faithful give life to those who listen, but the lies of the deceitful causes pain. [25]

The awe of the Divine builds up confidence, and makes the world safe for your children. [26]

The love of Divine Law is a wellspring of life. [27]

The glory of a leader is his growing population, but for a lack of people is a would-be leader's downfall. [28]

He who is slow to anger has great wisdom, but he who has a quick temper will surely make known his unconsciousness. [29]

A positive attitude adds years to one's life, but a negative attitude is like cancer to the bones. [30]

He who makes it hard for the poor brings shame to his Creator, but he who helps those in need honors Him. [31]

The unconscious creator experiences the results of his own misdeeds, but the person who understands Divine Law secures his place forever. [32]

Wisdom resides in the heart (*subconscious mind*) of those who have understanding, but an unconscious creator's thoughts are soon exposed. [33]

Goodness exalts a nation, but corruption is a shame to any people. 34

The leader's favor is toward a discerning servant, but his anger is toward the one whose actions cause shame. 35

Divine Insights

Chapter 15

A gentle answer turns away anger, but sharp word causes strife. [1]

An ingenious tongue uses wisdom in a good way, but the mouth of the unconscious speaks without understanding. [2]

The eyes of the Creator are in every place, watching the good and the bad. [3]

A gentle tongue is a fountain of life, but an unconscious tongue crushes the spirit. [4]

An unconscious creator turns away from the strong teaching of his father, but he who remembers the strong words spoken to him is wise. [5]

Great riches are in the house of those who acknowledge Divine Intelligence, but those who are unconscious experience lack, loss, and limitations. [6]

The lips of the conscious creator spread much learning, but with the unconscious this is not so. [7]

The Creator abhors the offerings of the unconscious, but the prayer of the faithful is His joy. 8

Divine Intelligence detests the ways of the unconscious, but He loves those who practice what is right and good. 9

He who turns from the right way will be confounded. He who hates correction will be destroyed. 10

Death and destruction are not hidden from the eyes of the Creator, how much more the thoughts of humanity? 11

A person who laughs at truth has no love for the one who speaks strong words to him. He will not seek out sound advice. 12

A glad heart makes a joyous expression, but when the heart is sad, the spirit is broken. 13

The mind of him who has understanding looks for much learning, but the mouth of fools' devourer ignorance. 14

All the days of the suffering are hard, but the joyous soul has a continual feast. 15

A little with the awe of the Creator is better than great riches with trouble. 16

A dish of vegetables with love is better than a gourmet meal with hatred. [17]

A person with a bad temper starts fights, but he who is slow to anger is a peacemaker. [18]

The path of the lazy person is overgrown with thorns, but the path of the faithful is a well-kept highway. [19]

A wise child makes his father proud, but an ignorant child grieves his mother. [20]

Foolishness is a joy to him who lacks understanding, but a person of understanding walks circumspectly. [21]

Plans go wrong without wise counsel, but in a multitude of counselors, plans are established. [22]

To give a good answer is a joy to a person, and how pleasing is a word given at the appropriate time. [23]

The path of life leads upward for the conscious creator, so he may keep from the torment of the lower consciousness. [24]

Divine Intelligence will end the house of the proud, but He will make a place for the widow. [25]

The Creator overturns the plans of the unconscious, but the words of the pure are pleasing to Him. 26

He who gains wealth by dishonest means brings trouble to his family, but he who will not be bribed will succeed in life. 27

The person who behaves wisely, before his Creator thinks before he speaks, but the mouth of the unconscious is a well of depravity. 28

The Creator is far from the unconscious, but He hears the prayer of those who think and behave appropriately before Him. 29

A smile on the face brings joy to the spirit. Good news is health to the bones. 30

He whose hears and listens to words of correction will live among the wise. 31

He despises himself who does not listen to words of correction, but he who receives strong correction gains knowledge. 32

The awe of the Divine Intelligence is the genius of the conscious creator, and humility comes before honor. 33

Divine Insights

Chapter 16

The desires of the soul belong to the person, but the answer of the tongue is from Divine Intelligence. [1]

All the ways of a person are pure in his own eyes, but Divine Intelligence weighs the thoughts, imaginations, and the intents of the heart (*subconscious mind*). [2]

Trust your work to Divine Intelligence and your plans will prosper. [3]

The Creator has made all things for His own plans, even the unconscious for the Day of Judgment. [4]

Everyone who is proud will experience shame. They will surely be disgraced. [5]

Loving-kindness and truth paid our debts in full. The love of Divine Intelligence restrains one from inappropriate behavior. [6]

When the ways of a person are pleasing to Divine Intelligence, even his enemies will be at peace with him. [7]

A little earned through honest endeavors is better than great wealth earned illegally. [8]

The thoughts of a person plans his way, but Divine Intelligence shows him what to do. 9

The lips of the leader speak as an oracle of Divine Intelligence; he should not stray from that which he knows to be right. 10

The Divine Law is an honest balance and a guaranteed scale; all the weights in the bag are its handy work. 11

It unacceptable for leaders to practice what is wrong. For a nation is built on what is right. 12

Lips that speak truth are the joy of a leader. Loved is he who speaks the truth in love. 13

The anger of a leader carries death sentence, but a wise person will appease it.14

Life is in the light of a leader's face, and his favor is like a cloud bringing the spring rain. 15

To get wisdom is much better than getting gold. To get understanding is to be preferred over silver. 16

The road to genius begins with turning away from erroneous thoughts. He who watches his over his behavior protects his life. 17

Pride comes before destruction and a prideful spirit comes before a fall. [18]

It is better to be humble of heart among poor, than to divide riches among the proud. [19]

He who is attentive to Divine Law will find abundance, and prosperous is he who trusts in Divine Intelligence. [20]

The wise-hearted are people of good sense: and people are persuaded by pleasing words. [21]

Understanding is a well of life to him who has it, but to correct an unconscious creator is a waste of time. [22]

The spirit of the conscious creator has power over his mouth and adds learning to his lips. [23]

Pleasing words are like honey. They are sweet to the soul and healing to the bones. [24]

There is a way that seems right to a person, but its end is the way of death. [25]

A person's hunger inspires him. The need of his mouth encourages him. [26]

A worthless person looks for trouble. His words are like raging fire. [27]

An ignorant person causes trouble. One who hurts people with rumors separates good friends. [28]

A violent person encourages his neighbor to violence, and leads him down a road that is going nowhere. [29]

He who winks his eyes is planning to do something inappropriate. The person who remains silent gives his consent to wrong behavior. [30]

Graying hair is a crown of glory. Those who think and behave appropriately before their Creator will experience a prosperous life. [31]

He who controls his temper is better than a Five-Star General. He who rules his emotions is better than one who captures a foreign country. [32]

Man makes decisions by rolling dice or tossing a coin, but outcome is determined by Supreme Intelligence. [33]

Divine Insights

Chapter 17

A stale piece of bread with peace and quiet is better than a house full of food with resentment. [1]

A servant who behaves wisely will rule over a son causing shame, he will share the inheritance as one of the family. [2]

The melting pot is for silver and the hot fire is for gold, but the Creator tests heart. [3]

An unconscious creator listens to others who are unconscious. A liar listens to words that are not beneficial. [4]

He who laughs at the poor brings shame to his Maker. He who is glad at others calamity will experience the equivalent. [5]

Grandchildren are the pride and joy of old men and a child is proud of his father. [6]

Fine speech is not becoming to an ignorant person; still less is false speech to a leader. [7]

A gift shared in secret is a magic token in the hands of him who gives it; wherever he turns, he prospers. [8]

He who forgives an error discovers favor. He who tells secrets separates best of friends. 9

A person of understanding learns more from being told the right thing to do than an unconscious creator learns from being severely discipline. 10

A person who will not obey Divine Law seeks trouble. So one who has no pity will be sent against him. 11

A person meeting a bear robbed of her cubs is better than meeting an unconscious creator in his thoughtlessness. 12

If a person returns negativity for good, he will continue to attract negativity into his life. 13

The beginning of contention is like opening a faucet. So stop arguing before fighting breaks out. 14

Both he who says that wrong is right, and he who says right is wrong, contradict Divine Intelligence. 15

It does an idiot no good to try to purchase wisdom, when he lacks understanding. 16

A friend loves at all times. A brother is born to share in difficulties. 17

A person without thinking makes promises, and becomes a co-signer for what another person owes. 18

He who loves drama enjoys causing trouble. He who opens his door wide looking for trouble will find it. 19

He who has a wayward imagination finds no good thing. He who has an undisciplined tongue experiences trouble. 20

A senseless child causes heartache, and the father of an unconscious child experiences no joy. 21

A positive attitude concerning life is good medicine for the soul, but a negative spirit is cancer to the bones. 22

An unconscious creator accepts bribes in order to pervert justice. 23

Those who have understanding experience wisdom, but the unconscious are left wanting though they search the world over. 24

An unconscious child is a sorrow to his father and trouble to the one who gave him birth. 25

It is not good to penalize those who acknowledge Divine Intelligence, and it is wrong to penalize faithful people for their integrity. [26]

He who is careful in what he says has much learning, and he who has a quiet spirit is a person of understanding. [27]

Even an unconscious creator, when he shut his mouth, is considered wise. When he keeps silent, he is thought to be a genius. [28]

Divine Insights

Chapter 18

He who isolates himself for his own private purpose goes against all good sense. [1]

An unconscious creator does not find joy in understanding, but only in voicing his opinion. [2]

With the unconscious creator comes contention, and where there is no honor, there is shame. [3]

The words of a person's mouth are deep waters. Wisdom comes like a flowing river exuding a pleasant sound. [4]

It is not good to favor the unconscious, or to keep what is right from the conscious. [5]

The lips of the unconscious manifest trouble and their words cause pain. [6]

The unconscious creator is destroyed by his own mouth, and he is ensnared by the words of his own lips. [7]

The words of one who speaks about others in secret are like delicious bites of food. They go down into the inside parts of the body. [8]

The lazy person is a brother to him who uses destructive words. 9

Divine Intelligence is a strong tower. The person who does what is right turns to Him and is protected. 10

The wealthy person's money is his strong city, and he trust it is like a high wall. 11

A person's pride will destroy him, but a humble person is honored. 12

Anyone who gives an answer before he hears the question is an idiot and will be embarrassed. 13

A positive attitude will help a person through his sickness, but who can bear a negative attitude? 14

An open mind grows in understanding and the ears of the conscious creator listens for much knowledge and understanding. 15

A person's gift makes room for him, and brings him in front of great people. 16

The first to tell his story makes people think he is right, until the other comes and refutes the story. 17

Tossing a coin puts an end to disputes and keeps powerful rivals from fighting. [18]

A brother who has experienced emotional hurt is harder to be won than a strong city, and he will be imprisoned by his arguments justifying his state. [19]

A person's stomach will be filled with the fruit of his mouth. He will prosper by the words of his lips. [20]

Life and death are in the power of the tongue and those who love it will eat its fruits. [21]

He who finds a wife finds a good thing, and gets favor from Divine Intelligence. [22]

The poor person seeks mercy, but the rich person responses harshly. [23]

A person who seeks friends must be friendly, but there is a friend who is closer than a sibling. [24]

Divine Insights

Chapter 19

An impoverished person who walks in her integrity is better than an unconscious creator who is perverse in her speech. 1

It is not good for a person to be without much learning, and he who hurries with his feet rushes into trouble. 2

The mindless behaviors of the unconscious causes destruction, because he imagines futile devices against his Creator. 3

Wealth adds many friends, but a poverty mindset separates best friends. 4

A person who tells lies about someone else will be disgraced. He who tells lies will be imprisoned by his own words. 5

Many will seek the favor of a philanthropist, and every person is a friend to him who is a giver. 6

When you have an impoverished mindset, even your family avoids you. Your best friends do not want to deal with you. If they see you coming, they walk the other way and act as if they did not see you coming. 7

He who gets wisdom loves his own life. He who cherishes understanding will discover wisdom, wellness, and wealth. 8

A person who tells lies about someone else will suffer the effects he sought to cause. He who tells lies will experience lack, loss, and limitations. 9

It is not right for an unconscious creator to live in great comfort, and for sure, for an ignorant servant to rule over great people. 10

A person of understanding is slow to anger. It is to his honor to forgive and forget a fault caused by another. 11

The leader's anger is like the growling of a lion, but his favor is like the morning dew. 12

A rebellious child breaks his parents' hearts. The arguing of a wife is like leaky faucet dripping all the time. 13

Houses and riches are an inheritance from parents, but an understanding wife is a gift from Divine Intelligence. 14

Laziness causes one go into a deep sleep, and a lazy person will experience lack, loss, and limitations. 15

He who keeps Divine Law keeps his soul, but he who does not will perish. [16]

Kindness shown to the poor is a blank check given to the universe, and the universe pays back those loans in full with interest. [17]

Instruct your child while he is young, and do not be discourage because of his tears. [18]

An angry person will experience the consequences of his anger, if you save him from himself, you will only have to do it again. [19]

Listen to words of instruction and accept correction, so that you may experience a life of wisdom, wellness, and wealth. [20]

The schemes imagined by people are many, but in the end, only the plans of Divine Intelligence will succeed. [21]

Everyone desires success, but it's better to be poor than to compromise one's values. [22]

The love of Divine Intelligence leads to wisdom, wellness, and wealth, and he who has it will sleep well, and will not be moved by circumstances. [23]

The worthless person is so lazy that he will not take the food from the bowl and place it in his mouth. 24

Strike a person who laughs at truth and the unconscious may become conscious. However, speak strong words to one who has understanding, and he will increase in wisdom. 25

He who hurts his father and puts his mother out of the house is a child who causes much shame. 26

My child, do not listening to advice that will cause you to turn away from truth. 27

A worthless person who tells all he knows laughs at sound advice, and the mouth of a gossiper spreads lies. 28

Judgment awaits those who laugh at the truth, and the unconscious will experience the results of their own causation. 29

Divine Insights

Chapter 20

People behave like idiots under influence of alcohol. Excessive drinking causes fights. Whoever is deceived thereby is not wise. [1]

The anger of a leader is like the roar of a lion. He who makes him angry forfeits his own life. [2]

It is an honor for a person to keep away from strife, but an unconscious creator is quick to argue. [3]

The lazy person does not plow before winter. Therefore, he begs during the time of harvest. [4]

The intentions of the heart (*subconscious mind*) are like water in a deep well, but a person of understanding draws it out. [5]

Every person brags about his own achievements but a sincere person who can find. [6]

How prosperous are the children of a person who acknowledges their Creator and walks in honor. [7]

A conscious leader who sits in judgment discovers deception with his eyes. [8]

Who can say, "I have cleansed my thoughts, and I am pure from any wrong behavior?" [9]

Divine Intelligence hates the deceptive practices of switching price tags and padding the expense account. [10]

You will know a child by his actions and they will prove if his ways are pure and right. [11]

Supreme Intelligence made both the hearing ear and the seeing eyes. [12]

Don't love sleep, or you will become improvised. Open your eyes and you will be filled with abundance. [13]

"It cost too much, it cost too much," says the customer, but when he goes away, he brags about his great bargain. [14]

There is gold and precious stones of great worth, but the lips of much learning are priceless. [15]

Secure a person's possessions when he becomes collateral for someone else's loan. In addition, hold him accountable when he secures a loan for another in a distant land. [16]

Stolen bread seems sweet to a theft, but later his mouth will be filled with sand. [17]

Make plans by listening to the wisdom of others and wage war by listening to wise counsel. [18]

Gossiper makes secrets known. Stay away from them, if they talk about others they will talk about you. [19]

A disrespectful child will experience an early death. [20]

A large inheritance does not guarantee an abundant life. [21]

Do not say, "I will repay wrong." Wait on Supreme Intelligence, and He will take care of it. [22]

The Divine Intelligence abhors fraud and deception. [23]

Divine Intelligence decides a person's steps. How can anyone understand his own way? [24]

It is dangerous for a person to make a promise to Divine Intelligence without thinking and then have second thoughts. [25]

A conscious leader removes the unruly from their positions and makes them pay for their inappropriate behaviors. [26]

The spirit of a person is the lamp of his Creator. It reveals the intent of his soul. [27]

A leader will stay in power as long as he is faithful and true. He can stay in his place if he does what is right and good. [28]

The honor of young men is their strength. Moreover, the honor of old men is their gray hair. [29]

Positive discipline shapes a child, and correction purifies his imagination. [30]

Divine Insights

Chapter 21

The imagination of the leader is like rivers of water held in the hands of the Divine Source. He turns it where He wishes. [1]

Every person's way is right in his own eyes, but Divine Intelligence knows the intent of the heart. [2]

To do what is right, good and fair is more pleasing to the Creator than gifts given on the altar in worship. [3]

Eyes lifted high and a proud imagination is a perversion in the eyes of Divine Intelligence. [4]

The goals of diligent lead to wisdom, wellness, and wealth, but all who scheme to get rich will be improvised. [5]

Riches gain by a deceit is like an empty cloud, and leads to lack, loss, limitations. [6]

The misdeeds of the unconscious will destroy them, because they refuse to do what they know is right. [7]

The way of an unconscious creator is perverse, but the actions of the pure in spirit are right. 8

It is better to live in a corner of a house than live in a mansion with an angry person. 9

The unconscious' desire is inappropriate. His neighbor finds no favor in his eyes. 10

When the person who laughs at the truth experiences heartache, the unconscious creator grows in wisdom. When a conscious creator is taught, she gains understanding. 11

The person who behaves wisely considers the outcome of the unconscious, and the unconscious are destroyed. 12

He who shuts his ears to the cry of the poor will cry himself and not be heard. 13

A gift in secret placates anger. A sincere gift quiets rage. 14

When justice flourishes, it brings joy to those who acknowledge Divine Intelligence. However, it fills the unconscious with fear. 15

A person who strays from the way of understanding will take his place in cemetery of the unconscious. 16

The person addicted to pleasure will be empty. The soul of the thrills seeker will never be satisfied. [17]

The unconscious creator is a ransom for those who acknowledges Divine Intelligence, and the unfaithful for the faithful. [18]

It is better to live in a tent than in a house with an angry person. [19]

There is wisdom, wellness, and wealth in the house of the conscious creator, but an unconscious creator wastes them all. [20]

He who follows what is right and loving and kind finds life, right-standing with the Divine Source and wisdom, wellness, and wealth. [21]

A wise person traverses the barricades of the powerful, and confounds that in which they place their trust. [22]

He who controls his thoughts, words, and actions preserves his life. [23]

"Proud," "Self-important," and "One who laughs at the truth" are the names of the person who acts disrespectful and prideful. [24]

The desire of the lazy person will kill him, because he refuses to work. 25

The lazy person is filled with desire all day long, but the person who acknowledges Divine Intelligence gives his best effort. 26

The gift of the unconscious is a despised thing. How much more when he gives it with false motives. 27

A person who tells a lie about someone else will be destroyed, but the words of a faithful person will be established forever. 28

The facial expression of the unconscious creator shows his deception, but a conscious creator displays confidence. 29

No human wisdom can stand against Divine Intelligence. 30

Men design of weapons for war, but the victory belongs to Divine Intelligence. 31

Divine Insights

Chapter 22

Desire a good reputation over great wealth. Divine favor is better than silver and gold. 1

The rich and the poor meet together. Divine Intelligence is the maker of them all. A conscious creator sees trouble and conceals, but the unconscious go on, and is destroyed. 2-3

Wisdom, wellness, and wealth are the rewarded to the humble of heart and to those who are in awe of their Creator. 4

Difficulties and obstacles await the unconscious, but the person who is mindful of her behavior will escape them all. 5

Train child according to his genius, and he will experience lifelong success. 6

The rich rule over the poor, and the borrower is indebted to the lender. 7

He who plants deceitful seeds will reap the harvest, and his cruel schemes will be discovered. 8

Those who are generous will prosper, because they share their wealth with the poor. 9

Conflicts and disputes will be resolved once you get rid of the naysayers. 10

He who exemplifies purity of thoughts, and whose speech is gracious, will reside in the company of great people. 11

The eyes of Divine Intelligence preserve those with understanding, but He will overturn the actions of the skeptic. 12

The lazy person will devise any excuse not to work, even saying, "There is a wild animal outside! I will be killed in the streets!" 13

The mouth of an unfaithful woman is a bottomless pit. The person who ignores his Creator shall fall therein. 14

Immaturity is deeply-rooted in the heart of a child, but positive discipline will guide him in the right direction. 15

The person who increases his wealth by stealing from the poor and giving to the rich will become impoverished. 16

Gems of Genius

Turn your ear and hear the words of the wise, and open your mind to what they teach. My words will be pleasing if you keep them in your heart, so they may be ready on your lips. I have taught you today, even you, so that your trust may be in Divine Intelligence. Have I not written to you great things of wise teaching and much learning to show you that the words of truth are sure, so you may give an appropriate answer to him who sent you. [17-21]

Do not rob the poor because he is poor, or crush those who suffer at the gate. The Creator will stand by the poor and help them, and will take the life of those who rob them. [22-23]

Do not have anything to do with an angry person, or go with a person who has a bad temper. Alternatively, you might learn his ways and get yourself into trouble. [24-25]

Do not be among those who make promises and become cosigners for what others owe. If you have nothing with which to pay, why should you give your bed for another? [26-27]

Do not remove the landmarks, which your fathers have put in place. [28]

Do you see a person who is excellent at his work? He will stand before great people. He will serve the elite. [29]

Chapter 23

When you sit down to eat with a leader, think about what is in front of you. Put a knife to your neck if you are a person who is given to overeating. Do not desire his special foods, for they are there to deceive you. 1-3

Do not labor to be rich. Stop trying to get things for yourself. When you set your eyes upon it, it is gone. For sure, riches make themselves wings like an eagle that flies toward the heavens. 4-5

Do not eat the bread of a selfish person. Do not desire his food. What he thinks in his heart (*subconscious mind*) he manifests in his life. He says to you, "Eat, drink, and be marry!" But he doesn't seek your best interest. You will vomit up the food you have eaten, and waste your compliments on deaf ears. 6-8

Do not speak in the company of an idiot, for he will abhor the wisdom of your words. 9

Do not take away the inheritance, or go against those without a father. For the One who saves them is strong. He will stand by them and fight their cause against you. 10-11

Open your mind to instruction and your ears to words of wisdom. [12]

Correct a child if he deserves it. If you discipline him, he will live. Discipline him promptly, and save him from his own misdeeds. [13-14]

My child, if you are wise in your thoughts, my soul will be pleased. My heart will be full of joy when your lips speak what is right. [15-16]

Do not be jealous of unconscious people; instead walk in the way of Divine Love. Know that you have the manifestation of your desire. [17-18]

Listen, my child, and be wise. Lead your thoughts in the right way. Do not be with those who drink too much alcohol or over eat. For the person who over indulge in drinking and eating will become impoverished, and too much sleep will cause a person to become destitute. [19-21]

Listen to your father who gave you life, and do not despise your mother when she is old. [22]

Purchase truth, and do not sell it, get wisdom, knowledge, and understanding. [23]

The father of one who acknowledges God will have much joy. He who has a wise child will be glad in him. Let your father and mother be glad, and let her who gave birth to you be full of joy. 24-25

Give me your heart, my child. Let your eyes find joy in my ways. For a woman who sells the use of her body is like a deep hole. An unconscious woman is a narrow well. She lies in wait as an armed robber, and causes many men to become unfaithful. 26-28

Who has trouble? Who has sorrow? Who is fighting? Who is complaining? Who is hurt without a reason? Who has eyes that have become red? Those who spend long hours at the bar drinking alcohol. Those who indulge in drinking mixed drinks. Do not look at wine when it is red, when it shines in the glass, when it is smooth in going down. In the end, it bites like a snake. It stings like the bite of a snake with poison. Your eyes will see strange things. Your imagination will think the wrong thoughts. Moreover, you will be like one who lies down in the center of the sea, or like one who lies above a ship's sail. "They hit me, but I was not hurt. They beat me, but I did not know it. When I awake, I will seek another drink." 29-35

Divine Insights

Chapter 24

Do not be jealous of unconscious people. Do not desire to be with them. For in their thoughts they make plans to harm others. Their lips conjure up trouble. 1-2

By wisdom, a house is built. According understanding, it is made strong, and by much learning, the rooms are filled with invaluable riches. 3-4

A wise person is strong. A person of much learning adds to his strength. For by wise counsel leaders make war, and sound advice secures great battles. 5-6

Wisdom is too hard for the unconscious to understand. He does not open his mouth in the gate. He who plans to do wrong will be known as a trouble maker. Planning to do a stupid thing is trouble, and the person who laughs at the truth is despised by the wise. 7-9

If you are weak in the day of trouble, your strength is small. 10

Save those who are being taken away to death. Keep them from being killed. If you say, "See, we did not know this," does not He who knows what is in the heart (*subconscious mind*) see it? Does not He who keeps watch over your soul know it? And will He not pay each person for his work? [11-12]

My child, eat honey, for it is good. Yes, the honey from the comb is sweet to your taste. Know that wisdom is like honey to the soul. If you find it, there will be a future, and your hope will not be destroyed. [13-14]

Unconscious creator, do not lie in wait against those who acknowledge their Creator. Do not destroy their resting place. For a person who acknowledges Divine Intelligence falls seven times, and rises again, but the unconscious falls in times of trouble and does not rise again. [15-16]

Do not rejoice when the one who hates you falls. Do not let your heart be glad when he slips. Divine Intelligence will see it and will not be pleased and will turn away His judgment from him. [17-18]

Do not worry because of those who do wrong, and do not be jealous of the unconscious. For there will be no future for the unconscious creator. The lamp of the unconscious will be extinguished. [19-20]

My child, honor your Creator and your leaders. Have nothing to do with those who are given to rebellion. For their trouble will rise up all at once, and who knows greatness of their destruction? 21-22

Additional Gems of Genius

These also are sayings of the wise. It is not good to show favor in judgment. He who says to the unconscious, "You are right and good," will be spoken against by people and abhorred by nations. However, those who correct the unconscious will find joy and good will come upon them. To give the right answer is like a kiss on the lips. 23-26

Complete your work outside and prepare your fields. Then after that, build your house. 27

Do not speak against your neighbor without a reason, and do not lie with your lips. Do not say, "I will do to him as he has done to me. I will pay him back for what he has done to me." 28-29

I passed by the field of the lazy person, by the grapevines of the person lacking wisdom. And saw it was all grown over with thorns. The ground was covered with weeds, and its stone wall was broken down. When I saw it, I pondered it. I looked and received insight. "A little sleep, a little rest, a little folding of the hands to rest," and your impoverishment will come as a thief, and your need like an armed robber. [30-34]

Divine Insights

Chapter 25

Genius Insights

These also are wise sayings of Solomon, which were written down by the men of Hezekiah, ruler of Judah. [1]

It is God's prerogative to conceal a matter, but it is the genius of leaders to discover it. [2]

The heaven above, and the earth beneath, so the genius of a wise leader enigmatic. [3]

Take away the impurities from the silver and a silver cup shall be fashioned from the remains. Take the unconscious away from the leader and his government will stand on what is right and good. [4]

Do not honor yourself in front of a leader, and do not stand in the place of great people. It is better to be told, "Come up here," than to be put down in front of a leader whom you admire. [6-7]

Do not be quick to debate your case. Or, what will you do in the end, when your neighbor puts you to shame? Argue your side of the problem with your neighbor, but do not tell the secret of another. Otherwise, he who hears you may put you to shame, and ruin your reputation. [8-10]

A word spoken at the right time is like a priceless jewel of set in the purest of gold. A wise person speaking strong words to a listening ear is like an earring of gold for the ear and a beautiful gift made of fine gold. [11-12]

A faithful person who carries news is like the ice cold cup of water in the summer time to those who send him, for he makes the spirit of his owners feel renewed. [13]

A person who brags too much of a gift he does not possess is like storm clouds without rain. [14]

When one is slow to anger, he wins the hearts of leaders. A gentle word has the power to shatter bones. [15]

Have you found honey? Eat until you are satisfied or you may eat too much and become ill. [16]

Do not spend too much time in your neighbor's house, or he may become tired of you and despises you. [17]

A person who tells a lie against his neighbor is like a heavy stick, a sword, or a sharp arrow. [18]

In time of trouble, trusting in an unfaithful person is like a bad tooth or a foot out of joint. [19]

He who sings songs to a heavy heart is like one who steals another's coat on a cold day, or one who pours alcohol on an open wound. [20]

If the one who hates you is hungry, feed him. If he is thirsty, give him water. If you do that, he will become ashamed of his actions, and Divine Intelligence will bless you. [21-22]

The north wind brings rain, and a hurtful tongue brings an angry look. [23]

It is better to live in a corner of the roof than to share a mansion with an angry woman. [24]

Good news from a distant land is like cold water to a thirsty soul. [25]

A well-meaning person, who interferes with an unconscious person, is like a well of mud or poisoned water. [26]

It is not good to eat much honey, or to seek self-glory. [27]

A person who cannot rule his own emotions is like a city whose walls are broken down. [28]

Divine Insights

Chapter 26

Like snow in summer and like rain during harvest time, so honor is not fitting for the unconscious person. [1]

Like a sparrow in its traveling, like a swallow in its flying, so inappropriate words said against someone without cause. [2]

A whip is for the horse, leather ropes are for the donkey, and a stern reprimand for an unconscious person. [3]

Do not respond to an ignorant person according to his foolishness, or you will be believed to be like him. Give an ignorant person a foolish answer, or he will believe that he is wise in his own eyes. [4-5]

He who sends a letter by the hand of an unconscious creator cuts off his own feet and brings trouble upon himself. [6]

A wise saying in the mouth of fools is like the legs of a disabled person who cannot walk. [7]

He who gives honor to an unconscious creator is like one who throws a stone on a rock pile. [8]

A wise saying in the mouth of fools is like a thorn that goes into the hand of a person who drinks too much alcohol. [9]

He who hires an unconscious creator is like a person who uses a knife and accidentally injures himself. [10]

An unconscious creator who repeats a negative action is like a dog that turns back to lick up what he has thrown up. [11]

Do you see a person who is wise in his own eyes? There is more hope for an unconscious creator than for him. [12]

The lazy person says, "There is danger on the way! There is trouble in the streets!" As a door turns, so does the lazy person on his bed. The lazy person buries his hand in the dish. It makes him tired to bring his hand to his mouth and eat. The lazy person is wiser in his own eyes than seven geniuses who can give a wise answer. [13-16]

He who passes by and interferes in someone else's fight is like one who takes a dog by the ears. [17]

Like an insane person who discharges a gun into a crowd of people, so is the person who deceives his neighbor with a lie, and says, "I was only joking." [18-19]

When there is no wood, the fire goes out. Where there is no one gossiping, arguing stops. An arguing person makes matters worse. He is like coals to burning wood and gasoline to a fire. The words of one who tells secret things about other people are like good-tasting morsel of food. They go down deep inside the body. [20-22]

Scandalous lips and the mind of the unconscious creator are like a refining pot covered with silver dross. [23]

He who hates covers it up with his words, but stores up false ways in his heart. When he speaks with kindness, do not believe him, for there are seven things that are despised in his heart. Even if his hate is covered with false ways, his deception will be uncovered in front of an audience. [24-26]

He who digs a deep hole will fall into it, and he who rolls a stone will have it return upon him. [27]

A lying tongue despises those it harms, and a mouth that speaks false words destroys those who are deceived by it. [28]

Divine Insights

Chapter 27

Do not boast about tomorrow, for you do not know what a day will bring. [1]

Let another person praise you, and not your own mouth. Let a stranger, and not your own lips. [2]

A stone is heavy, and sand is heavy, but a person angered by an unconscious creator is heavier than them both. [3]

Anger causes trouble and a bad temper is like a flood, but who can stand when there is jealousy? [4]

Sharp words spoken in public are better than love in secret. [5]
The painful rebuke given by a friend is faithful, but the kiss of an enemy is deceitful. [6]

A person with a full stomach loathes honey, but even bitter things are sweet to a hungry person. [7]

Like a bird that goes away from her nest, so is a person who goes away from his home. [8]

Oil and perfume make the heart glad, so are a person's words sweet to his friend. [9]

Do not leave your friend or your father's friend in times of need, and do not go to your brother's house in the day of your trouble. A neighbor who is near is better than a brother who is far away. 10

Be wise, my child, and make my heart glad, so I may answer him who attempts to puts me to shame. 11

An enlighten person sees trouble and hides, but the unconscious goes on and are destroyed. 12

Take the person's coat that has cosigned for what a stranger owes. Moreover, hold him to his promise that has made a vow on the behalf of an irresponsible woman. 13

The irresponsible person is cursed for praising his neighbor too early in the morning. 14

An arguing woman is like dripping water on a rainy day. Trying to restrain her is like trying to stop the wind, or like trying to keep a hand full of oil from running through your fingers. 15-16

Iron sharpens iron, so one person sharpens the intellect of another. 17

He who cares for the fig tree will eat its fruit, and he who tends to the needs of his employer will prosper. [18]

As water acts as a mirror to a face, so a person's beliefs reflect the person. [19]

Just as the cemetery never has enough bodies, the eyes of the unconscious creator are never satisfied. [20]

The melting pot is for silver and the fire for gold, and a person is tested by his ability to receive praise. [21]

Although you crush an unconscious person emotionally to dust, he will not depart from his thoughtless behavior. [22]

Know well how your flocks are doing, and keep in mind the condition of your cattle. Riches do not last forever, and wealth does not pass from generation to generation. When the grass is gone, the new plants are seen, and the plants of the mountains are gathered up. The lambs will be for your clothes, and the goats will bring the price of a field there will be enough goats' milk for your food, for the food of your entire house, and food for your servants. [23-27]

Divine Insights

Chapter 28

The unconscious run away when no one is chasing them, but those who acknowledge God have great strength and the heart of a lion. [1]

A rebellious country has many leaders. However, a wise and knowledgeable leader brings stability. [2]

A leader who makes it hard for poor is like a heavy rain that destroys the harvest. [3]

Those who turn away from God support the ungodly, but those who understand Divine Law contest them. [4]

Unconscious people do not understand what is right and fair, but those who look to Divine Law understand all things. [5]

Better to be poor and honest than to be rich and a liar. [6]

He who keeps Divine Law is a wise, but person who does not control his appetite brings shame to his father. [7]

He who becomes wealthy through extortion gathers it for him who is kind to the poor. 8

He who turns his ear away from listening to Divine Intelligence, even his prayers are despised. 9

He who leads good people into error will fall into his own deep hole, but good will come to those who are blameless. 10

The rich person is wise in his own conceit, but the poor person who has understanding sees through him. 11

When those who acknowledge God win, there is great honor, but when the unconscious rule, people hide themselves. 12

It will not go well for the person who hides inappropriate behavior, but the person who confesses his fault will receive mercy. 13

Prosperous is the person who always acknowledge Divine Intelligence, but person who hardens his heart will experience difficulty. 14

The unconscious rule the poor like a ferocious lion or an angry bear. 15

A leader who steals from the impoverished lacks understanding. But he who despises dishonest gain will prolong his life. 16

A person who is guilty of murder will flee for his life. Let no one help him. He who blameless will be protected, but he who is unconscious will fall without a warning. 17-18

He who works his plan will have wisdom, wellness, and wealth, but he who wastes time will become impoverished. A faithful person will prosper, but he who chases get rich schemes will suffer lost. 19-20

To show favor is not good, because a person will sale his soul for a piece of bread. 21

The desire of the unconscious creator is to rush to be rich. He does not know that poverty will overtake him. 22

He who speaks strong words to a conscious creator will later find more favor than he who gives insincere lips service. 23

He who steals from his parents, and says, "I did nothing wrong," is the friend of a person who causes devastation. 24

An arrogant person starts brawls, but all will go well for the person who places his trust in his Maker. 25

He who trusts in his own imagination is an unconscious creator, but he who walks in wisdom is protected. [26]

He who gives to the poor will lack no good thing, but calamity will overtake the person who shuts his eyes to the needy. [27]

When the unconscious rule, people hide themselves, but when they die, those who do what's right multiply. [28]

Divine Insights

Chapter 29

A person who does not listen to constructive criticism will be destroyed suddenly and will not be rescued. [1]

When those who acknowledge God rule, the people are glad, but when an unconscious creator rules, the people have sorrow. [2]

A person who loves wisdom makes his father glad, but he who goes with prostitutes waste his inheritance. [3]

The leader makes the land strong by doing what is right and fair, but the one who accepts bribes destroys it. [4]

A person who flatters his neighbor with deceit spreads a net for his own feet. [5]

An unconscious creator is trapped by his actions, but a person who acknowledges God sings a joyful song. [6]

The person who acknowledges God cares about the rights of poor, but the unconscious creator does not understand such things. [7]

Corrupt person bring a city to ruin but the enlighten person appeases anger. [8]

When a conscious creator argues with an unconscious creator, only the unconscious creator shows emotions, and there is no peace. 9

The violent abhor those who acknowledge God, but a good person cares for his life. 10

An unconscious creator always loses his temper, but a conscious creator holds his peace. 11

If a leader listens to lies, all who work for him will become deceitful. 12

Divine Intelligence gives insight to both the poor and the deceitful person. 13

If the leader is fair as he judges the poor, his government will stand forever. 14

Discipline and strong words give wisdom, but a child who gets his own way brings shame to his mother. 15

When the unconscious are many, errors are multiplied, but those who acknowledge Divine Intelligence will see their fall. 16

Correct children when they error and they will bring you comfort. Yes, they will bring joy to your soul. 17

Where there is no vision, the people perish: but he that keeps Divine Law will prospers. [18]

An ignorant employee will not be trained by words; though the meaning is clear to him, he will not pay attention. [19]

Do you see a person who is quick with his words? There is more hope for an insane person than for him. [20]

He who gives good care to his servant from the time he is young, will in the end discover a son. [21]

An angry person starts fights, and a person with a bad temper attracts trouble. [22]

A person's pride will bring him down, but he whose spirit is without pride will receive honor. [23]

Whoever is an accomplice of a thief is an enemy of his own soul. He will not testify, even under oath. [24]

A person is entrapped by his fear, but he who trusts Divine Intelligence will prosper. [25]

Many seek a leader's approval, but true favor comes from Divine Intelligence. [26]

An unconscious person is a shame to those who acknowledge Divine Intelligence, and he who acknowledges Divine Intelligence is a shame to the unconscious person. [27]

Divine Insights

Chapter 30

The Genius of Agur

The wise saying of Agur the son of Jakeh of Massa. The man says to Ithiel and Ucal:

"For sure, I am more ignorant than any man, and I do not have the understanding of a man. I have not learned wisdom, and I do not know much about the Holy One. Who has gone up into heaven and come down? Who has gathered the wind in His hands? Who has gathered the waters in His coat? Who has put in place all the ends of the earth? What is His name, and what is His Son's name? For sure you know." 1-4

Every word of God has been proven true. He is a safety-blanket to all who trust in Him. Do not add to His words, or He will speak strong words to you and prove you to be a liar. 5-6

Two things I have asked of You. Do not keep me from having them before I die: Take lies and what is false far from me. Do not let me be poor or rich. Feed me with the food that I need. Then I will not be afraid that I will be full and turn my back against You and say, "Who is the Creator?" And I will not be afraid that I will be poor and steal, and bring shame on the name of my God. 7-9

Do not speak against an employee while talking with his employer, or he may speak against you and cause trouble. 10

There are those who curse their fathers, and do not honor their mothers. There are people who are right in their own eyes, but are not washed from their own dirt. There is a kind, O, how proud are his eyes! His eyes are opened wide with pride. There is a generation whose teeth are like swords, and their jaws like knives, to devour the poor from the earth, and the needy from among people. 11-14

The parasite has two daughters, "Give," "Give." There are three things that are never filled, four that never say, "Enough": The place of the dead, the woman who cannot have children, the earth that is always thirsty for water, and fire that never says, "It's enough." 15-16

The eye that makes fun of a father and hates to obey a mother will be picked out by the ravens of the valley and eaten by the young eagles. 17

There are three things which are too great for me, four which I do not understand: The way of an eagle in the sky, the way of a snake on a rock, the way of a ship out at sea, and the way of a man with a woman. 18-19

This is the way of a woman who is not faithful in marriage: She eats and washes her mouth, and says, "I have done no wrong." 20

Three things that cause the earth to shake and four things it cannot stand: an ignorant servant when he becomes a leader, an ignorant person filled with food, a woman unloved by her husband, and a servant who controls her employer's affairs. 21-23

There are four things that are small on the earth, but they are very wise: The ants are not a strong people, but they store up their food in the summer. The badgers are not a strong people, but they make their houses in the rocks. The locusts have no leader, but they go as an army. You can take the lizard in your hands, but it is found in leaders' houses. 24-28

There are three things which have honor in their steps, even four which show honor in their walk: The lion, which is powerful among wild animals and does not turn away from any, the proud rooster, the male goat, and a leader with his army. 29-31

If you have been ignorant in honoring yourself, or if you have planned wrong, put your hand on your mouth. Churning milk makes butter, and hitting the nose brings blood. So fighting comes because of an angry person. [32-33]

Divine Insights

Chapter 31

The Genius of Kings

The words of Lemuel king of Massa, which his mother taught him:

What, my son? What, son who came from within me? What, son of my promises? Do not give your strength to women, or your ways to that which destroys kings. It is not for kings, my child Lemuel, it is not for kings to drink wine, or for kings to desire strong drink. Or they might drink and forget their Creator, and go against the rights of all who are suffering. Give strong drink to him who is ready to perish, and wine to him in bitter distress. Let him drink and forget his lack, loss and limitations. Open your mouth for those who cannot speak, and for the rights of those who are without hope. Open your mouth. Be right and fair in your decisions. Stand up for the rights of those who are unable to stand for themselves. 1-9

Who can find a good wife? She is worth far more than rubies that make one rich. The heart of her husband trusts in her, and he will never stop getting good things. She does him good and not bad all the days of her life. She looks for wool and flax, and works with willing hands. She is like merchant ships that trade. She brings her food from far away. She rises while it is still night and makes food for all those in her house. She supplies the young women with work. 10-15

She gives careful thought to land and purchases it. She plants grapevines from what she has earned. She makes herself ready with strength, and makes her arms strong. She sees that what she has earned is good. Her lamp does not go out at night. She creates products by hand. She gives to the poor, and reaches out to those in need. She is not afraid of the snow for those in her house, for all of them are dressed in red. She makes coverings for herself. Her clothes are linen cloth and purple. Her husband is known in the city, when he sits among the leaders of the land. She makes linen clothes and sells them. She brings belts to those who trade. Her clothes are strength and honor. She is excited about the future. She speaks with wisdom. The teaching of kindness is on her tongue. She looks out for the well-being of those in her house, and she does not waste time. Her children rise up and honor her. Her husband does also, and he praises her, saying: "Many daughters have done well, but you have done better than all of them." Charm is deceitful and beauty fades, but a woman who trusts in God will be greatly praised. Give her the fruit of her hands, and let her works praise her throughout the world. 16-31

Divine Insights

About the Author

DeCarlo A. Eskridge is a spiritual life-coach/trainer, host of Blogtalk Radio's "Live Your Greatness," motivational speaker, certified hypnotherapist, certified N.L.P. practitioner/trainer, author, business owner, and minister. He is very proud to have authored and independently-published several books through his company NU DAE Enterprises where he serves as President and CEO.

A prolific teacher and encourager, DeCarlo A. Eskridge reads over 50 books a year, and listens to countless hours of audio programs. He is a Certified Life Coach through Franklin Covey and a motivational speaker who earned advanced honors at Toastmasters International. He is also an Ordained Minister with over 25 years of biblical study.

DeCarlo A. Eskridge has been imbued with an inexhaustible, unyielding, and unrelenting thirst and hunger for knowledge. His mission is to travel the globe teaching, empowering, inspiring, and transforming the lives of millions with the truths he has discovered in order that every person recognizes who he or she is, what he or she can accomplish, and that they live it!

THE BLACK BOOK
NU DAE Enterprise Publications

DeCarloEskridge.com

ISBN-13: 978-1469981871
ISBN-10: 1469981874

Made in the USA
Charleston, SC
26 May 2012